THE PERFECT INTERVIEW

Max A. Eggert
MA, BSc, AKC Psykol, FIPM, MITD

Max Eggert first read Theology at King's College London before transferring his allegiance to Psychology at Birkbeck, from there to Industrial Relations at Westminster and then back to further clinical training in the Department of Psychiatry at Sheffield University.

Having enjoyed a successful career in HR and General Management within the engineering, construction and electronics sectors, he decided in 1984 to pursue his professional passion in career work assisting consultancies set up in the then new area of support called Outplacement.

Since then, Max has assisted many thousands of executives and managers to become successful in their careers through his consultancy Transcareer in the UK and at Interim in Australia where he is Chief Psychologist.

Max has two adult children, lives in Bondi Beach in Australia, and Hackney in the UK. His current research interests include clinical hypnosis for personal empowerment, and his other consuming passion is riding his thoroughbred, 'Splinter'. As an Anglican Priest, Max is licensed in the Dioceses of Sydney and Chichester as an NSM.

OTHER TITLES IN THE SERIES

The Perfect Appraisal Howard Hudson
Perfect Assertiveness Jan Ferguson
The Perfect Business Plan Ron Johnson
The Perfect Career Max Eggert
Perfect Communications Andrew Leigh and Michael Maynard
The Perfect Conference Iain Maitland
The Perfect Consultant Max Eggert and Elaine van der Zeil
Perfect Counselling Max Eggert
Perfect Costumer Care Ted Johns
The Perfect CV Max Eggert
Perfect Executive Health Dr Andrew Melhuish
Perfect Financial Ratios Terry Gasking
Perfect In-House Training Colin Jones-Evans
The Perfect Leader Andrew Leigh and Michael Maynard
The Perfect Meeting David Sharman
The Perfect Negotiation Gavin Kennedy
Perfect People Skills Andrew Floyer Acland
The Perfect Presentation Andrew Leigh and Michael Maynard
Perfect Relaxation Elaine van der Zeil
Perfect Stress Control Carole McKenzie
Perfect Time Management Ted Johns
The Perfect E-commerce Steve Morris
The Perfect E-mail Steve Morris
The Perfect M Commerce Steve Morris & Paul Dickinson
The Perfect Project Manager Peter Bartram
The Perfect Public Speaking Paul McGee

THE PERFECT INTERVIEW

All you need to get it right first time

Max Eggert

RANDOM HOUSE

BUSINESS BOOKS

This edition published in the United Kingdom in 1999
by Random House Business Books

9 10

First published in 1994 by Arrow Books
The Random House Group Limited
20 Vauxhall Bridge Road, London SW1V 2SA

Random House Australia (Pty) Limited
20 Alfred Street, Milsons Point, Sydney,
New South Wales 2061, Australia

Random House New Zealand Limited
18 Poland Road, Glenfield,
Auckland 10, New Zealand

Random House (Pty) Limited
Endulini, 5a Jubilee Road, Parktown 2193, South Africa

The Random House Group Limited Reg. No. 954009

ISBN 0 09 940618 7

Companies, institutions and other organizations wishing to make
bulk purchases of any business books published by Random House
should contact their local bookstore or Random House direct:
Special Sales Director
Random House, 20 Vauxhall Bridge Road, London SW1V 2SA

Tel: 020 840 8470 Fax: 020 828 6681

www.randomhouse.co.uk
businessbooks@randomhouse.co.uk

Typeset in Sabon by SX Composing DTP, Rayleigh, Essex
Printed and bound in Denmark by
Nørhaven Paperback A/S, Viborg

For
Max-Charles and Marisian,
for all the interviews they have given me
and for all the interviews they have to come.

Acknowledgements

My thanks to friends and colleagues with whom I have had the pleasure of working in the important area of Outplacement.

In the early days of Outplacement we all stole our ideas from each other but I stole most from Roy Perry, Sid Hilsum, Bill Huddleston, David Sagar, John Burton, Penny Swinburne and Andrew Hearsey.

Special thanks go to five gifted people without whom this work would not have got off the ground: Sian Eggert, Ros Spry, Ruth Graham-Pole, Kathy Parkes and Lucy Shankleman.

Gender Point
'He' and 'she' in this book are interchangeable. In writing, sometimes 'she' felt more appropriate than 'he' and sometimes the reverse was true.

Contents

Introduction   1

Part 1 – Preparation for the Interview
1 Preparation   9
2 Pre-conditioning the interviewer   10
3 Banish wooden legs   12
4 The first rule of being an interviewee:
   don't answer questions   13
5 Use a career statement   14
6 Talk to yourself   16
7 Up against the wall   18
8 Check the buzz   19
9 Affirmations   21
10 Interview structures   23
11 Assessment centres   27
12 USPs   31
13 Anticipate questions   32
14 The interview objective   33
15 Position yourself   35
16 Practise bragging   37

Part 2 – Looking and Behaving the Part
17 Looking the part   41

18 Looking good, be good   42
19 Dress: the basic rules   43
20 What to wear   45
21 Pick up clues   46
22 The handshake   47
23 Body language and NVCs   48
24 Are you sitting comfortably?   49
25 The chair, legs and hand positions   50
26 Look at the interviewer   52

Part 3 – The Interview Questions – and How to
Handle Them
27 The three super questions   55
28 Super question 1   56
29 Super question 2   58
30 Super question 3   60
31 Reduce their risk   62
32 The politician – or don't say anything until
    your brain is in gear   63
33 Stay above the line   65
34 Tell the story   67
35 Stress the benefits   69
36 Explain the gaps   71
37 No tentative language   73
38 How to be humble   74
39 The weakness question   75
40 Multiple questions   77
41 The topical question   79
42 Interests   81
43 Have you any questions for us?   83

Part 4 – The 100 Most Popular Questions
Asked by Interviewers
44 100 popular questions   87
45 50 likely interview questions for graduates   92

Part 5 – Managing the Interview Process
46 Interview start and finish 99
47 First & last: primacy & recency 101
48 The interview: arrive early 104
49 Divest 106
50 Watch the layout 108
51 Do not argue with the interviewer 110
52 What happens next? 112
53 Don't eat, drink, smoke or be merry 114
54 Staying silent 116
55 Avoid DTBs (Defensive Tactical Behaviours) 118
56 References 120

Part 6 – Getting the Best Deal: Negotiating Pay
and Conditions
57 Getting a better deal 125
58 Pay and conditions (the basics) 126
59 Pay negotiation strategies 128

Part 7 – After the Interview
60 Interview, review and learn 133
61 It helps to stay in touch 134
62 Interview yourself 136

Postscripts I to IV 137

Part 8 – Checklists
A Pre-interview planning 145
B The interview checklist 148
Feedback 149

Introduction

Over the past few years I have helped thousands of people get the job they wanted. For many people a major difficulty is that they are unskilled in presenting themselves. As a result, they do not always get the jobs they should. And the better people are at their jobs, the less frequently they go to interviews – only poor performers get lots of interview practice!

This book shows you how to present yourself and your skills in the best possible way. Research has shown that interviewers make up their minds very early on in the interview, and that personal chemistry between interviewer and interviewee is more powerful in influencing the recruiter's decision than anything the applicant has achieved! These and other research findings can be used to your advantage.

A GOOD START

Getting an interview is really good news for the job hunter. It means you are almost there. Most people approach an interview with trepidation, thinking of all the reasons why they should *not* get the job. We call these 'wooden legs'. Here are some of the more popular wooden legs:

I will not get the job because:

- I'm too old/young
- I'm not/too qualified
- I'm not/too experienced
- I've spent too much/little time in my present job

Whilst some anxiety is reasonable and healthy, to take all your wooden legs with you to the interview is just plain daft.

THE GOOD NEWS is:

1. You get an interview only if the interviewer thinks you can do the job on offer. Do you know any interviewer who would deliberately waste their time on no-hopers? Of course not. What you have achieved or not and how that relates to the job can be seen from your curriculum vitae. Thus your perceived 'handicaps' have already been accepted as presenting no significant problem.
2. Not every applicant is seen. Most shortlists consist of only five or six people, so you have a one in six chance of being selected. Now you have to work out what it was in your application or CV that made you attractive to the interviewer and plan how to maximise your strong points.
3. Strange as it may seem, research suggests that interviewing is one of the most unreliable management techniques. This can work to your advantage: you can train yourself to present the best possible picture of yourself and your accomplishments. It is important always to tell the truth in an interview but, with forethought, rehearsal and good preparation you

can present what you have to offer in the most positive and attractive way.

4. The majority of managers have not been trained in interviewing skills. This is particularly true of line managers and senior executives. This puts you in an ideal situation to assist your interviewer gain the information you wish to give about yourself. Once you have read, practised and acted on the suggestions in this book, you will know more about interviewing than most interviewers. You will be able to enjoy an interview with a professional interviewer and assist those who are not very competent.

Will the interviewer mind you being so skilled? No, it will be a pleasant experience for him or her to interview someone who is so well prepared.

5. You are in total control of the information you give about yourself. The interviewer asks the questions, but you decide how to answer them and what information you will release. The professional interviewer is trained to ask open questions, such as

- Tell me about yourself?
- What do you enjoy in your job?
- Why did you leave that company?
- What brings you here?

All these questions can be answered in a variety of ways depending on what you choose to say and what information you decided to give.

6. With a little thought and planning you can decide what questions you will be asked. Most interviewers are human – they have doubts and concerns, hopes

and fears like everyone else. Look at your application and/or CV through their eyes. Think about their organization and the requirements of the position on offer and then ask yourself 'What questions would I ask?', 'What would my reservations be if I was considering this application for the position and my job depended on it?' (Just think what happens to interviewers who keep hiring the wrong candidate!) Having run through this process you can anticipate the questions and prepare appropriate answers. But remember you must always tell the truth.

No one would run a marathon without training and being sure of the route. As an interviewee, you can train and know the route from your armchair – well, almost!!

In this book there are lots of tips and hints to help you secure the job and/or the promotion you want. An interview, like an examination, is not the fairest or the best way to make judgements about people, but for most managers it is the only method they have. This book will help you to present yourself in the best possible way to help them make the right decision about you.

There are eight major sections:

1: Preparation for the interview
This is to help you prepare for the interview. It will provide you with an understanding of what an interview is from 'the other side of the desk' and ways of looking at yourself from an interviewer's point of view.

Most interviewers naturally focus on meeting their own needs. This part of the book helps you to recognize the employer's viewpoint and needs.

2: Looking and behaving the part
Interviewers have so little information upon which to

make selection decisions that how you look and behave has far more significance than it deserves. This section will help you present yourself in the best possible way.

3: The interview questions – and how to handle them

The main skill of the interviewer is to ask questions. If you cannot answer them appropriately then your chances of success are minimal.

This section will help you understand why different types of questions are asked.

4: The 100 most popular questions asked by interviewers.

These are the most popular questions that interviewers ask. Work through them and you will be ready for any interview.

5: Managing the interview process

It is not what you do that matters, but the way that you do it. This section helps you understand the context of the interview and how best to deliver your answers to the questions.

6: Getting the best deal

There is no point in getting the job and not being rewarded appropriately. This section covers how to negotiate the best deal that your new employer can afford.

7: After the interview

Some more ways of helping yourself get selected even after the interview is over.

8: Postscripts and checklists

Further ideas and lists to help you succeed.

PREPARATION FOR THE INTERVIEW

PART ONE

PREPARATION FOR THE
INTERVIEW

CHAPTER 1

Preparation

Job offers are won or lost on the thoroughness of the preparations you make for the interview. Before the employer sees you a lot of work has gone into drawing up job targets, job descriptions and person specifications as well as thinking through start rates, reviews and induction arrangements. Some firms, appreciating how costly the wrong appointment can be, will invest significantly in training all those associated with the selection process. You must match this preparation.

Just as you would not run a marathon without a lot of preparation, so the wise applicant will not approach the interview without getting 'interview fit'. Here is how . . .

CHAPTER 2

Pre-Conditioning the Interviewer

It is well established that the expectations of the interviewer about the candidate formed during the pre-interview stage can be self-fulfilling. Interviewers who expect to encounter a strong candidate treat that candidate differently during the interview from the other applicants. The interviewer who expects good answers or positive responses will create opportunities for the candidate to perform well.

Consequently, anything you can do to create the right impression will be valuable. Here are a few ideas:

- A professional-looking CV emphasizing your achievements
- A well-written application form which refers to your CV and/or emphasises your strengths
- A strong covering letter detailing how closely you match the job specification and your USPs (see page 31)
- A positive letter confirming the interview arrangements and how much you are looking forward to the meeting

If the interviewer expects you to be good you will sense

this favourable attitude and be encouraged to try even harder to present your strengths. So help the interviewer help you – use the pre-conditioning strategy in presenting yourself strongly beforehand so that you are perceived to be the best candidate.

CHAPTER 3

Banish 'Wooden Legs'

It is surprising how many people prepare themselves to fail the interview. These are the wooden legs I mentioned earlier and here's a reminder of how they work:

- I'm too old/young
- I'm too experienced/inexperienced
- I'm over/under qualified
- I'm male/female, etc.

What you should remember is that as you have achieved an interview, your interviewer has accepted whatever limitations you put on yourself. Like everyone else, an interviewer's time is expensive. He or she will invest it in you only if you think you can do the job, so do not be too concerned about your wooden leg – whatever it might be, it is not a problem.

PS: I actually worked with a storesperson of some ten years' duration who thought her artificial leg limited her chances of employment. She now works for a major bank in a clerical capacity!

CHAPTER 4

The First Rule of Being an Interviewee: Don't Answer Questions

This might come as something of a surprise, but it is one of the most powerful pieces of advice given. Interviewers eat the answers they are fed, so as the interviewee, you must not say anything unless you are prepared to speak to it or expand on what you have said.

The best advice I can give is:

Do Not Answer Questions – Respond to Them

In this way you can control the information you release about yourself. In the interview situation, you are 100 per cent in control of what you say. Interviewers can work only on the information you *give* them, so give them the very best information about yourself.

Dr Kissinger once greeted the press corps with the words 'Which of you have questions for my answers!'

He knew what information he wanted to release on that occasion and you would do well to be in the same position at an interview – knowing what information you wish to release about yourself.

CHAPTER 5

Use a Career Statement

If you know exactly what sort of job you want or you are going for, then develop a career statement about yourself. This should be used as early as possible in the interview.

A career statement has the advantage of creating the right expectations in the mind of the interviewer, preparing him or her for the information that is to come later.

Here are some examples:

- I am a highly motivated buyer with a proven record of successful negotiating in technical and commercial settings
- I am a young and determined professional, with experience across the wide range of insurance product knowledge, experienced in both sales and marketing of new business and skilled in man management

The statement should be brief and powerful, highlighting all your employment 'trump cards', including skills from previous jobs which, if left to be gleaned from your career history, would not be given enough prominence in the context of the particular job you applied for.

Work on a career statement can also help answer those open questions which usually occur during the early part of the interview. The question: 'Tell me about yourself' is a gift to the well-prepared statement.

CHAPTER 6

Talk to Yourself

No, not the first sign of madness, but an important part of getting through the interview.

You use different parts of your brain for thinking and talking. Have you ever had that experience of knowing what to say and yet somehow not being able to get it out of your mouth? At any interview, you are bound to feel some anxiety and this will not improve your fluency.

In our society it is not done to be a self-publicist, so all of us are a little out of practice in talking about ourselves, our work and our achievements. Yet the interview is structured specifically for you to do just that. Keep asking yourself those open questions -How, Why, What and Tell me – and answer them to yourself.

Practise talking about yourself out loud – in the bath, whilst driving – others might think you rather strange, but who cares if you are more likely to get the job!

Research suggests that those who are fluent are rated as:

- More intelligent
- Having better interpersonal skills
- Making better managers

So practice, and develop your fluency for talking about your achievements.

CHAPTER 7

Up Against the Wall

Suppose you were invited to participate in a rather different recruitment procedure. Your prospective employer lines up all the potential candidates and says, 'Each of you has just 30 words to say who you are and depending on how you answer, I will make a choice.' What would your 30 words be?

In fact, it is a very good discipline. Ask yourself: What am I selling/offering this prospective employer? What do I have that they want and need to help make them more successful?

Prepare the '30-word statement' as an exercise and you will find it transforms your interview chances.

The 30-word statement will do at least two things. First, it will make you think about exactly why an employer should hire you. Second, you will have a quality control mechanism for all that you say in the interview because, unless is supports your 30-word statement, it is best left unsaid. Remember, the employer wants you for your contribution to the organization.

All that you say in the interview should amplify your 30-word statement.

CHAPTER 8

Check the Buzz

This is particularly good advice for those who have been out of work for a time or those who wish to move from one sector of employment to another, from manufacturing to, say, retailing.

Management activity, just like clothing, goes through 'fashions'. Recent 'fashions' have included:

- Management by Objectives
- :erial Resource Planning
- Quality Circles
- Putting People First
- Zero Based Budgeting
- The Pursuit of Excellence
- Total Quality Management
- Putting the Customer First

It is important for you to check the buzz for your prospective industry or sector. This is easily done by reading the journals for your sector and/or for your profession. Go back six months and skim through the journals so that you pick up current topics of concern and the buzz words and key phrases that are fashionable.

Wherever possible, use your network into your

prospective industry so that you can pick up information first hand. One job searcher I know actually rang several firms as a 'researcher' examining the major issues facing the industry that she was interested in entering.

In this way you will be better prepared to answer questions such as:

- 'What do you know about our industry?'
- 'As a manager, what issues are of interest to you?'
- 'What in your view should our organization be doing to improve our position?'
- 'What do you think we should be doing about the XYZ issue?'
- 'What major factors do you think are causing us concern right now?'

CHAPTER 9

Affirmations

Henry Ford said, 'If you think you can or if you think you can't, you're right.'

There is a great lesson here for interviewees because we limit ourselves by our self-image or self-concept.

This is particularly important if you are going for a bigger job with more responsibility but are not absolutely sure that you've got what it takes.

If you are unsure or your confidence level dips during the interview your interviewer will pick it up. Sometimes your attitude is even communicated non-verbally.

A way of overcoming this is to develop affirmations. These are brief statements about yourself in the present tense about what you want to be.

Examples
For a salesman:

'I am an international sales manager with excellent marketing and promotional experience'

For a Personnel Manager:
'I am a seasoned Personnel Director with a proven track

record of establishing good human resource support and systems in green field situations'

The interesting thing about affirmations is that you actually become what you affirm. This is because you become attracted to and interested in those things which support your affirmation, and you will develop relevant experience and skills. Having affirmations has a direct effect on your environment, yourself and your career.

So in interview terms we can adapt Henry Ford:

'If you think you are, or if you think you are not, you're right'

CHAPTER 10

Interview Structures

Interviewers are trained, not born! This means that you can have access to the same information.

Interviewers are trained in two major areas: how to ask questions and how to structure an interview. How to respond to the questions they are trained to ask is fully covered later in this book, but here let us examine interview structures.

Interview structures ensure that all significant aspects of the candidate are covered during the interview. For instance, it is no good offering a sales job to someone who cannot drive, a job in London to someone who lives in Newcastle and won't move, or a job in the defence industry to a pacifist.

If you know the structure then it will assist you in your preparation because you can anticipate the question areas. Also, during the interview if certain types of question are asked you will know which structure your interviewer prefers and thus be able to anticipate other areas the interviewer will be interested in. It is like playing contract bridge – you play much better if you and your partner understand not only your own system but also the system of your opponents!

There are two basic interview structures:

- The Seven Point Plan (by Alec Rodger)
- The Five Point Plan (by John Munro Fraser)

THE SEVEN POINT PLAN

This plan suggests that questions should be asked in the following seven areas:

- *Physical Aspects*. Does this person have the right health, build, physical charisma and impact for the job on offer?
- *Attainments*. Does this person have the right academic and professional qualifications (or equivalents) for this job?

  Does this person have the right experience and track record to be able to do this job? (60 per cent of the interview will be spent in this section.)
- *General Intelligence*. How intelligent is the person and how is their intelligence used in their work situation?
- *Special Aptitudes*. Does this person have any special aptitudes (spatial, linguistic, numerical, etc.) that are directly related to the job?
- *Interests*. How does this person spend their spare time/money and what it say about their potential skills and motivations at work?
- *Disposition*. What is this person's personality and what are the implications for the job?
- *Circumstances*. What effects have this person's circumstances had on their career to date and how will their present and future circumstances affect their performance in the job?

Sometimes candidates are asked questions which they feel are irrelevant, but if you know the structure you can understand what lies behind the question.

Would you take on a salesman for a highly competitive market if his interests were collecting stamps and breeding guppies?

Would you take on a cleaner whose brother was a professor, whose sister was a consultant brain surgeon and whose father a high court judge?

But many candidates feel that what they do outside work and what members of their family do are no concern of the interviewer.

THE FIVE POINT PLAN

Here the main categories are:

- *Impact on Others*. What kind of responses does this person's appearance, speech and manner bring out in other people?
- *Qualifications and Experience*. Does this person have the necessary knowledge and skill to undertake the work required?
- *Innate abilities*. How quickly and accurately does this person's mind work, and what are the implications for the job on offer?
- *Motivation*. What kinds of work appeal to the individual and how much effort is he/she prepared to apply to it?
- *Emotional Adjustments*. How well adjusted is this person to himself, his situation and his colleagues and what are the implications for the job?

Knowing the structure of the interview will help you to understand what the interviewer is looking for and also help him or her recognize it!

As a good preparation exercise, draw up a seven point plan for the particular job you are going for so that you can anticipate probable question areas and how you might deal with them.

CHAPTER 11

Assessment Centres

As early as 1949 a researcher named Wagner showed that the interview as an instrument of selection lacked both reliability and validity. His findings have been replicated frequently since then. Amongst the difficulties of the interview were that candidates were not asked the same questions and when they were asked the same question the answers required from the candidate were obvious. In an attempt to overcome this and other difficulties, selectors together with occupational psychologists have developed what are called Assessment Centres.

At Assessment Centres people, (usually in groups), have their abilities measured. There are usually four parts to the Assessment, namely:

1. Psychological Questionnaires attempting to measure individual abilities and personal traits
2. Group Activities to examine how individuals respond in group and/or problem-solving situations
3. Social Activities to see how candidates typically conduct themselves usually over a dinner and/or a plant tour – sometimes cynically called 'Trial by Sherry'
4. One-to-one or Panel Interviews by senior line managers

In this way the selectors can gain more and better information about a candidate. Also, candidates are observed in situations which are more like real work settings. However, even Assessment Centres are not perfect and it is possible to improve your performance significantly with a few simple techniques and strategies for Questionnaires and Social Activities.

PSYCHOLOGICAL QUESTIONNAIRES

It is not advisable to attempt to fake answers to questionnaires for two reasons. Firstly, if the organization is looking for a definite personality type and you massage your response to fit, it is unlikely that you will be successful. Secondly, if you do massage your scores the assessor is likely to pick up the fact that you are not telling the whole truth. In psychological terms this is called motivated distortion, where someone is trying to present a picture which is not a true reflection of him or herself.

Ability tests, however, are different. You cannot make yourself any cleverer than you are but there is a danger of achieving only a low score if you are out of practice. Just as a darts player is good at adding difficult number combinations because of sheer practice, so it is possible to develop IQ skills up to your full potential. Practice will not make you perfect, but it will help you achieve your personal optimum.

'How to' books on IQ are readily available and it is worthwhile working through one or two to get into the swing of solving problems. Just as if the assessment included a crossword, you would be wise to practise – you might not be able to solve *The Times* crossword in ten minutes, but practice would help. So with IQ questionnaires – you might not get into the top five per cent but you will still do better with practice.

GROUP ACTIVITIES

These usually take the form of a group discussion or problem-solving situation where the group, usually not more than eight candidates, is invited to reach a consensus solution.

The strategy in these situations, which are assessed by trained observers, is to have a good idea of what is being looked for in a candidate. The criteria may, for example, include skills in:

- Communication
- Judgement
- Reasoning
- Persuasiveness
- Problem solving

Candidates at an Assessment Centre should think through what likely characteristics are going to be examined by the observers so that when opportunities occur they can demonstrate their abilities.

It is important to make a *contribution* as the observers will otherwise have nothing to comment upon. You can be an active listen and a full participant but unless you contribute you cannot be assessed. Here are some simple strategies:

- Learn everyone's name in the group and use names as frequently as possible
- Summarize other people's positions before you give your own ideas or solutions

- Help the group understand you by giving reasoned arguments before you give your conclusions
- When appropriate, remind the group of the objective of the discussion or exercise
- When appropriate, remind the group of the time constraints for the exercise
- Find common ground whenever you can by highlighting areas of agreement and/or appealing to common values
- Towards the end of the exercise make summary statements when you can
- Make notes and take responsibility for being the scribe for the group, particularly when conclusions or solutions are being agreed

CHAPTER 12

USPs

USP is a sales term meaning Unique Selling Point. The concept behind the USP is that if there is a range of products of a similar type then a USP will ensure that your product is perceived as different, unique and better.

The concept can be used of candidates. If I shortlist, say, six candidates for a job from 100 or so applicants, each of the six will fit the person specification for the job. It is up to you as the applicant to be able to demonstrate your USP for the position on offer.

Pose the question to yourself: 'What have I got that I can offer which makes me special, or different from other candidates? What makes me fit? What are my USPs?'

Have you got special skills or experience which could get you closer to the job specification? Can you develop knowledge of the sector or job requirements?

Remember that the interviewer usually has to make a choice between candidates on the day; so the USP concept can be turned into a question for the candidate, e.g.:

'Tell me, why should I select you?'

It will be your USPs that help your selection.

CHAPTER 13

Anticipate Questions

No one is a perfect fit for any job. No one matches the person specifications in every respect. Any interviewer is going to attempt to identify and probe those areas of your background or experience where you are not up to the specification. These are the areas that put you (and your interviewer) at risk.

Before the interview itself you can prepare to be questioned on these problem areas.

Where you are a good fit as far as skills, qualifications or experience are concerned can be quickly examined and it should be easy for you to respond to close questioning on those area of your background.

However, you know yourself better than the interviewer does and you are best placed to know where you might fall below the standard, so it is important that you practise your answers. Anticipate how you will let the interviewer know that your apparent lack of skill or experience is not a problem, and emphasize the most relevant skill and experience that you *do* have. Remember, the interviewer already thinks you can do the job, otherwise you would not be there, so it is just a case of giving the right assurance.

CHAPTER 14

The Interview Objective

It is very important to be clear about what the objective of the interview is – it is not always, as you might expect, to get the job.

A useful saying is 'if you don't know where you are going, you will end up somewhere else'. This is true of the interview.

Your objective could be:

• To get on the shortlist
• To get to the interview with the line manager
• To find out if you want the job or to work for the organization

– a whole host of objectives are legitimate.

If you know what your objective is then you will be able to tailor your answers accordingly.

For instance, if your interviewer is from personnel, it will be a waste of time dazzling him or her with your technical ability. Far better to concentrate on your motivation and team orientation and values.

Before planning the interview, identify and write down your objective for the interview, namely:

- The objective of this interview is . . .
- So I must slant my answers towards . . .
- The points I wish to get across to achieve this objective are . . .

CHAPTER 15

Position Yourself

Some interesting research has suggested which is the best interview position to increase your chances of being selected.

According to the research, to be interviewed first is the worst. Managers do not interview often. Even personnel professionals do not interview all the time. Consequently it takes time to warm up and get up to interviewing speed. This is even more true of board interviews where there are a group of interviewers. It takes time to settle down, discover the right questions, and generally get into the stride of interviewing.

Almost as bad is being interviewed immediately after lunch or being the last person of the day to be seen. After lunch the interviewer is getting back into stride again and is not at his or her best. Interviews usually overrun, so the last interviewee is usually short-changed in terms of time and attention. It may not sound much, but a five-minute cut from a 40-minute interview reduces your chances of getting positive information across by 12.5 per cent. If all your fellow interviewees are as good as you, that is very significant.

Sometimes it is not possible to reschedule your interview time, in which case you have to rely on all the other strategies. However, it is always worthwhile telephoning to see if a change can be effected. The best position is the next to last for the day.

Sometimes candidates are given a choice of times. Choose well.

CHAPTER 16

Practise Bragging

It is part of our cultural heritage not to talk about ourselves and certainly not about our achievements. In the interview the selectors will not know how good you are unless you tell them. It is the job of the candidate to ensure that the interviewer's effort is kept to a minimum, so you must overcome this cultural tendency towards self-deprecation.

EXERCISE IN BRAGGING

Make a list of:

- 5 achievements
- 5 skills, or
- 5 things you are good at, or
- 5 things you are proud of at work

Then invite a colleague to strike off, at random, two from your list of five. You then have five minutes to persuade your colleague that the two items should go back on the list.

This exercise will provide excellent experience in

talking about yourself at a time when you were achieving or using your skills at work.

At the end of the exercise, your friend can tell you whether or not the item is allowed back on the list. The reasons you are given will be useful feedback.

You might also like to ask your friend if it sounded as if you were bragging. The answer usually given is 'No. You were just talking about what you did.'

Remember – interviewers will not know how good you are unless you tell them.

PART TWO

LOOKING AND BEHAVING THE PART

CHAPTER 17

Looking the Part

The way we present ourselves and the way we say things have long been know to be significant. Communication is far more than just the words we use. Alfred Adler said: 'If we want to understand a person . . . we have to close our ears. We only have to look. In this way we can see as in a pantomime.' Four centuries earlier, the advice 'not to watch a person's mouth but his fists' was attributed to Martin Luther.

In the selection institution the interviewer is so anxious to assess candidates that the significance of non-verbal messages is increased. Thus, interviewees must try to control the information about themselves which they communicate non-verbally.

In this section we cover the basics of dress and posture.

CHAPTER 18

Look Good, Be Good

Interviewers have limited information on which to base their final decision, so how you look has a tremendous influence on your success rate. Research strongly suggests that physical attractiveness influences selection, a phenomenon so well known that it is labelled Impression Management.

The older you are, male or female, the more important this becomes.

If you are out of work you have a golden opportunity to get fit and, more importantly, get to your ideal weight. Employers want people who are vigorous and have the stamina for hard work as well as being able to take stress.

From your CV or application form your interviewer will know how old you are, so age is not a major problem (otherwise your selectors would not be seeing you) but how old you *appear* and how fit you are will be significant.

If other things are equal, the job will go to the person who looks the fittest or appears in good health. Healthy people are attractive people so invest in yourself.

CHAPTER 19

Dress: The Basic Rules

Because the interviewer is usually the first person to see you from the company when you are seeking employment, how you dress is an important part of your impression management strategy. Of course, interviewers are more interested in what you can do and the skills you possess, but attention to one's clothes can and often does tip the balance. People perceived to be attractive and well-groomed generally receive higher ratings than applicants thought to be unattractive or inappropriately dressed. There is even evidence to suggest that more attractive employees achieve greater career success, so good appearance is generally advisable, not just for the interview.

Here are some basic rules for dress:

- Dress to suit yourself – style and colour – rather than high fashion
- Be traditional rather than avant-garde
- Dress as expensively as you can afford
- Darker colours are more powerful than lighter colours
- Get a good haircut
- Buy good shoes and keep them clean

- If you buy a new outfit practise wearing it before the interview
- Less rather than more jewellery
- Dress to the stereotype of the industry or function
- Co-ordinate your colours

What to Wear

Just as there are fashions in clothes, so there are fashions for styles and colours in organizations. In every organization there is an accepted style of dress.

Because the question 'Will this person fit in?' (see page 60) is dominant in the mind of the interviewer, the interviewee's fit with the corporate style tends to take on a considerable significance.

It is easy to get information on corporate style. First, visit the firm about lunchtime a few days before the interview and notice carefully what people are wearing in terms of style, colour and accessories.

The other source of information is the company's Annual Report which these days features an obligatory picture of members of the board.

Just ask yourself what is the predominant colour and style of clothing, colour of tie, length of hair, etc. You don't have to a be a clone to succeed in work but it might help you get through the interview!

CHAPTER 21

Pick Up Clues

It is impossible for any human to spend time in one place and not to alter the environment. Just as you create an impression by what you wear, so will an interviewer create an impression by the personal items in his or her office – from family photographs to golf trophies, from pictures to framed certificates. Is the office neat and tidy or cluttered and confused?

Office planners call them micro-environments. What does the office tell you about your interviewer and the organization? Can this information help you become empathetic to the interviewer? Does it mean you might present yourself or your information in a different way?

CHAPTER 22

The Handshake

There is no real connection between type of handshake and personality, but there is in the mind of many interviewers. There is so little information to go on about a candidate that anything is likely to be picked up and used, particularly at the beginning of the interview when the first impression is being created. So practise shaking hands firmly.

No one is going to give you a job on the basis of a handshake, but a good friendly and firm handshake may just contribute to the overall impression you wish to create.

CHAPTER 23

Body Language & NVCs

What we say with our bodies is very powerful, and you can increase your likelihood of success by ensuring that you give out positive non-verbal clues.

The major positive NVCs are as follows:

- A higher smile rate
- Nodding the head when the interviewer is speaking
- Leaning forward while listening and when replying
- A high level of eye contact (see page 52)

all of which deliver a positive message to the interviewer that you are important – which, of course, you are.

The result of all this is that you are more likely to be given a favourable rating than a candidate who does none or very few of these things. However, it is important not to overdo things and it would be sensible to practise.

CHAPTER 24

Are You sitting Comfortably?

Body language is thought to contribute over 60 per cent to the credibility of what people say, so in the interview situation it is very important to get this aspect correct.

Sit as far back in the chair as possible. If you sit on the edge of the chair because you are anxious, as you relax, and professional interviewers are trained in *rapport* skills, you will lean back awkwardly in the chair. Or if you are asked a difficult or challenging question your body sometimes recoils as if you had been physically hit. Questions such as:

- Why were you made redundant?
- Why did you not do better?
- Why did you fail?

and similar challenges are all likely to have this effect.

If you are sitting correctly you can avoid expressing anxiety in this way, and answer the questions easily and positively (see page 65).

The Chair, Legs and Hand Positions

THE CHAIR

Some interview settings are devised as if in preparation for a negotiation, with the chairs of the interviewer and the interviewee directly opposite one another ready for 'eyeball-to-eyeball' confrontation. This is not helpful because before you start you are forced into an unnatural situation: if you watch people who are friends and colleagues they tend to sit more to the side than opposite each other.

In the interview you can create a more relaxed situation by turning the chair 45 degrees when invited to sit down. This takes a little practice but can be done quite easily, and in itself displays great self-confidence: it is the interviewer's chair in the interviewer's room and you have moved it.

Now that the chair is positioned appropriately, you can show how much you like the interviewer by turning your trunk, head and shoulders towards him so that your shoulders are parallel to his. This will make you appear friendly, warm, receptive and empathetic.

THE LEGS

A 'low cross' or the 'athletic position' is appropriate.

High-crossed legs give the impression of defensiveness which is not appropriate. The athletic position is where your dominant leg is brought under your chair and only the toe of your shoe is touching the floor, while your non-dominant leg is firmly planted on the floor, parallel with the direction of the chair, with both the sole and heel of your shoe in contact with the floor.

This is a very powerful position – it makes you look as if you are ready for action.

The 'athletic position' is not the most suitable for women, who should position the legs in a low cross, or, keeping the legs together, just cross the ankles.

THE HANDS

Keep your hands lower than your elbows. Rest them on your thighs or clasp them in a low steeple. A steeple is where the fingers are dovetailed together with the thumb of your non-dominant hand resting on top of your other thumb. (A high steeple is when the hands in the steeple position are brought higher than the elbows – not so powerful.)

The steeple position is useful for those who fidget or who are likely to flap their hands or arms about when they speak. A rough rule in body language is that the less people move their hands and arms, the more powerful they are. This is because they are used to being listened to and they do not have to resort to gesticulation to get their message across. The technical term for this is Low Peripheral Movement (LPM); so when being interviewed, maintain LPM and you will look even more impressive.

CHAPTER 26

Look at the Interviewer

It is important for you to look the interviewer in the eye because this will make you appear more confident.

Research carried out in 1978 identified a positive relationship between qualification for a position and eye contact. Those that had good qualifications but made no eye contact were considered to lack self-confidence and thus be less suitable. Would you put someone in a job who appeared to lack confidence? Of course not, so at the interview look the interviewer in the eye.

Why just at interview? Why don't you practise this anyway? It may even help you in your current business and social life.

Some people have difficulty looking at others 'eye-ball-to-eyeball', and if you are one of these, then practise looking at the interviewer's ear. If he or she is more than a metre away they will not be able to tell you are not looking at them. Again, this means practice, so start as soon as possible.

THE INTERVIEW QUESTIONS – AND HOW TO HANDLE THEM

PART THREE

THE INTERVIEW QUESTIONS
— AND HOW TO HANDLE
THEM

CHAPTER 27

The Three Super Questions

The good news is that interviewers ask only three basic questions. All their questions fall into one of three general areas which are the major concerns of the selector:

- CAN THIS PERSON DO THE JOB?

- WILL THIS PERSON DO THE JOB?

- WILL THIS PERSON FIT IN?

Let us examine them one by one.

CHAPTER 28

Super Question 1

CAN THIS PERSON DO THE JOB?

This question is about experience, track record, achievements – in short what you have done.

At least 60 per cent of a professional interviewer's time with you will be spent on assessing your experience and how suitable you are for the appointment.

Throughout the interview your interviewer will be asking herself: Has this person got the experience and skills we need to make a contribution to the job on offer?

It is up to you to take any question and respond in such a way that you can deliver information about your skills and experience, e.g.:

- *'What was it like at xyz?'*
  It gave me an opportunity to do abc and efg. One of the many projects I worked on was hij . . .
- *'What sort of person do you like to work for?'*
  Looking back over my bosses, I enjoyed working with Mrs Smith because with her I was able to do abc, etc.

- '*What direction do you see your career taking?*'
  Well, I have good experience in abc and skills in efg
  so I would obviously like to develop them in . . .

The beauty of being asked open questions (see page 16)
is that you can use them to get across the information
you think most appropriate.

CHAPTER 29

Super Question 2

This is the second of the basic questions asked by interviewers. When you have answered super question 1 appropriately the selector will know that you have both the ability and the experience to do the job on offer. You can do the job – but will you? So the second super question is:

'WILL THIS PERSON DO THE JOB?'

It is obvious that this question is about your dispositional aspects and your approach to work. How hardworking are you? How motivated, committed, loyal, etc. – all the aspects which convince your potential employer that you will do more than just fulfil your contract. This is the selection equivalent of the retail slogan 'Service with a Smile'. It is that additional commitment to personal excellence, which indicates not only that you are able to do something but the positive way that you will do it.

You can choose to answer most questions about your work and career from this perspective. For example.

58

Q. *What was it like at ABC Co?*

A. It was interesting. Like all jobs the work fluctuated but at ABC you couldn't predict when. So it was necessary to be highly flexible, work within changing parameters and, on more than one occasion, stay late and work at weekends.

As you can see, the question could have been answered in terms of ABC's product, market position, management style, technology, etc., but by choosing to answer in terms of 'Will this person do the job?' you have responded to the question. You have begun to address a major concern of the selector.

In preparation for your interview, decide which aspects of your work to date illustrate that you are committed and motivated – that you give more than most. Once you have prepared these illustrations you will be amazed at how often the interviewer will provide you with questions that furnish an opportunity to address this point.

CHAPTER 30

Super Question 3

Now you have shown you have the ability and the motivation, there is only one area left to cover, but an important one. If birds of a feather flock together, then executives of corporations clone together, so Super Question 3 is:

'WILL THIS PERSON FIT IN?'

It really does not matter how good you are; unless you fit the company image you are unlikely to get the job.

Organizations are like individuals in that they have character and value systems. Two companies can make the same product but be completely different in their world view. If values are the concern of the organization, and are represented by the organizational persona, it must follow that the company attracts to itself employees who share those values.

The more senior you are in organization, the more important fitting in becomes. At interview, provided you agree with the value system of your potential employers, it is very important for you to take whatever opportunities they may give you to show how you can fit in.

There are four major areas where the value system operates:

- How people are managed and power is distributed
- How jobs get done
- How people relate to one another and how they are motivated
- How competition is handled in the market place

By reading company literature, and by active listening to employees, including the nuances of the interviewer, you can pick up clues in these vital areas.

Important Note:
If you find yourself at variance with your potential employer's value system you would do well to consider any job offer very carefully. It is very difficult to be successful in a culture to which you feel an outsider. There is more to career success that just technical competence.

CHAPTER 31

Reduce Their Risk

Have you thought what happens to interviewers who keep getting it wrong? They become interviewees themselves. In a way, each time an interviewer sees an interviewee he puts his job on the line. The interviewer's own career success is based upon making the right decision about candidates, so you can help him or her by reducing the risk.

The process is essentially an easy one to master. As the interviewee, you ask yourself, 'Why am I being asked this question?'

'What is the area of concern of the interviewer? How can I lower the anxiety that lies behind the question? In short – how can I reduce the risk?'

Your role is to choose the best information you have about yourself and give it.

Just as you select clothes from your wardrobe according to where you are going, with different clothes for work and for holidays, in the same way you select the appropriate topics from the wardrobe of your career.

Each experience should be specially selected to reduce the risk of the interviewer. Ensure that by your selection you not only enhance your career chances but also those of your interviewer.

CHAPTER 32

The Politician – or Don't Say Anything Until Your Brain is in Gear

Having got this far in the book, you will know that every question the interviewer asks has a purpose and that it is unwise to answer until you know:

- The reason for the question
- The most appropriate answer
- How to reply positively (see page 65)

This may sound a tall order but in fact it is very easy because of the wonderful mechanism between our ears called the brain, which can process at a deep level something like 1,500 concepts a minute and process language at about 600 words a minute. Most people speak at about 100 to 120 words a minute, so there is a lot of spare capacity which you can use to your advantage, especially with difficult questions. Do what the politicians do – say nothing until your brain is in gear. Here is an example:

- Interviewer: *What is the biggest problem you have had to overcome at work recently?*

(This is a nasty question since, when you talk about a problem, even if it is not one of your own making, because if something called Attribution Theory the interviewer will hold you partly responsible.)

So you have to play the politician and reply:

- *Interviewee*: Thank you, that is an interesting question because I have had, generally speaking, such a good year. However, if I reflect over the last few months . . . let me see . . . Yes, there was one problem which was useful because I learnt so much from it. The situation was . . .

In the 15 seconds it would take you to say the above, you should have been able to work out:

- The reason for the question
- The most appropriate answer
- How to reply positively

One of the easiest ways to fail in an interview is to give a knee-jerk reaction to a well-placed question. Now you understand the principles of 'the politician' you can work out variations for yourself. A word of warning – don't over-use this little tactic.

- Interviewer: *How old are you now?*
- Interviewee: That is an interesting question because . . .

It just won't do you any good!

CHAPTER 33

Stay Above the Line

Research suggests that negative information attracts supplementary questions. Good news tends to be accepted at face value.

Also, negative information is more easily remembered than positive information – perhaps because this type of information is being sought by the interviewer.

The answer is simple: ALWAYS TALK ABOVE THE LINE

Think of your career as a horizontal line. This represents time. On the left put another line at right angles. This is your success line.

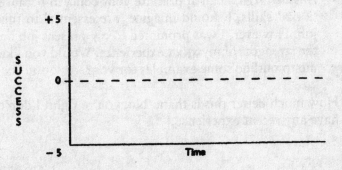

Figure 1

From 0 to +5 is the level of your success and from 0 to −5 is the level of your missed opportunities. Everyone's career has ups and downs. So here is a career line.

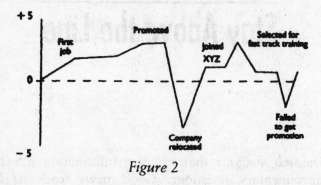

Figure 2

No one has a perfect career but as you are talking about yours you can choose to release only the positive information. Always talk 'above' the line. If you are forced below the line then respond to the questions as briefly as possible and lead your interview back above the line.

For example:

- Question: *But you don't have any recent experience?*
- *Answer*: Yes, I can appreciate your concern because 'xxxx' skills, I should imagine, are essential to this job. However, I was promoted to my present job on the strengths of my xxxx experience. Would you like me to outline some examples for you?

How much better this is than, 'No, you're right, I don't have any recent experience.'

CHAPTER 34

Tell the Story

Interviewers are trained not to ask hypothetical questions of the 'What would you do if?' variety. The reason is that imagined behaviour is significantly different from actual behaviour. Certainly, it would be rare in an interview for someone to volunteer negative information about himself or his skills.

To assist interviewers to deal with reality rather than future fantasy there is a technique called the Patterned Behaviour Description Interview (PBDI). This quite simply asks candidates 'Can you think of a time when you . . .?' or 'It says on the your CV you are . . . Can you talk about an actual example where this was significant?' In terms of real information about a candidate this is far more powerful because you the candidate are talking about real events and what you actually did, not what you think you might/would do.

It is not necessary for you to wait for an interviewer trained in PBDI techniques. Wherever possible tell the story.

Stories are remembered much more readily than adjectives or traits which are applied to individuals. So for a question such as 'How would you describe yourself?' you can reply, 'Fair, creative and hard-working' but where is the evidence? Much better would be a 'When I' story, e.g., 'When I was at Myers I was responsible for all their PR and there was a problem with image so I changed all our publicity material and the result was 24 per cent increase in new clients. So I suppose you could say I was creative and hard-working'. What makes this powerful is that it is a real situation which speaks for itself. Also, the story is more easily remembered.

In your preparation for the interview, work on your real life stories. Do not exaggerate your role or your contribution, but make it as interesting as possible. It was Lord Byron who said, 'The best prophet of the future is the past' so by telling stories of the past you will be telling your prospective employer what you will be doing for them in the future.

CHAPTER 35

Stress the Benefits

There is an old adage in sales which says 'You see the sizzle, not the sausage'. In other words, it is the benefit that is bought, not the feature. For example, you might be the best Field Service Engineer there is, but that is not why you are hired. It is because your skills mean minimum downtime. It is the latter which is the real reason for hiring you.

In thinking about your achievements at work, it is always useful to ask yourself the question 'Who benefited from my work and in what way?' Then, when talking about yourself your statements can become what is known as benefit-laden. For example, 'In 199x I exceeded my sales target by 20 per cent (feature) which meant that the company continued to dominate the market (benefit).'

Sometimes it is not easy to identify a benefit. One way is to ask 'So what?' 'So what was the result?' 'So what did this mean?' 'So what could the company now do?' These questions will help you identify the benefit.

It may sound harsh, but employers are far more interested in what you can do for them than in what skills or abilities you have as an individual. The interviewer is trying to establish what benefits you might bring to the organization and where those benefits outweigh those of other candidates.

Present yourself as a benefits package to the interviewer.

It takes a little practice to put together but use phrases such as:

- . . . which means that . . .
- . . . which resulted in . . .
- . . . so that . . .
- . . . the benefit was . . .
- . . . we gained because . . .
- . . . the advantage was . . .

Think of such phrases as hinges which link your feature – a skill or an experience – to the benefit it brought to the employer.

CHAPTER 36

Explain the Gaps

Customs & Excise officers working in the Green Channel are trained to look for the absence of the ordinary or the presence of the extraordinary because that is what makes people objects of suspicion.

Interviewers are not given the same intense training, but obviously in preparing to interview you they will be using the same sort of principles. What would you have expected in your career in terms of job moves and promotion given your qualifications and experience, and what has actually happened?

Doing exceptionally well will attract as many questions as not coming up to expectations.

'Pushes and Pulls' will be of particular interest. That is to say, what pushed you, or pulled out, out of one job or position and into another.

You must be prepared to talk about these areas because the professional interviewer will probe here for insights into your motivations, aspirations and value systems. Questions about your job will uncover your skills. Questions about the moves you made and why will reveal how you apply your skills and what sort of person you are.

Significant gaps between activities or jobs will attract

questions. What was the reason for the year off before university or the six-month gap in your employment record? The wise interviewee will think through suitable answers which can be delivered in a positive manner, e.g.:

- 'I wanted to travel and broaden my horizons so I planned and self-funded a working tour of North America. It was particularly useful because . . .
- 'If my career was going to develop in the way that I wanted, it was important for me to review my total situation, undertake a personal SWOT (Strengths, Weaknesses, Opportunties, Threats) analysis and then select the appropriate sector. I had several job offers which I turned down and that is why there was a three-month break. I'm very pleased I did it that way because . . .'

CHAPTER 37

No Tentative Language

Because of a cultural imperative not to push ourselves forward, when we speak about achievement we become self-deprecating and we communicate this in a variety of ways. One of the most damaging is the use of tentative language when talking about hopes and aspirations:

- I feel I could
- I think I can
- Perhaps I would

The use of 'I feel' weakens everything that follows it. There is a world of difference between 'I feel I could do a good job' and 'I could do a good job'.

It is the same with the phrase 'I think'. It dilutes your strengths and abilities.

By avoiding these tentative phrases your statement will sound far more powerful in the ears of the interviewer. Tentative language encourages a tentative response, but you want to achieve a very definite result.

If you have difficulty making strong 'I' statements about yourself – see the section on 'How to be Humble' (page 74) – and do the bragging exercise a few times with a friend. The interview is one of the few places where it is legitimate to promote yourself and one's abilities.

CHAPTER 38

How to be Humble

Because you are the subject of the interview's interest and, by now anyway, you should be talking as much as possible about your achievements (see page 37), it is difficult not to sound an egoist through the constant use of 'I': I did do this and I did that. Remember that it is more powerful to say 'I did' rather than 'We did', but there are some other strategies that can be employed by using such phrases as:

- People would say that I . . .
- Friends have told me that I . . .
- Colleagues are always saying that I . . .
- My boss once remarked that I . . .
- A reference would say that I . . .
- My experience shows that I . . .
- The record would show that I . . .

This is rather like getting a third-party reference and is always very useful in presentations to potential buyers. You are not actually blowing your own trumpet but getting the essential information about your achievements across to the interviewer in a more subtle way.

CHAPTER 39

The Weakness Question

If you get asked questions about your strengths then you will be asked about your weaknesses. This is difficult because you cannot say you do not have any nor can you say you used to be arrogant but now you know you are perfect!

We already know (see page 65) that negative information has a greater significance for interviewers than positive information, so candidates much be very careful indeed as to how they respond to this question.

Remember that you do not have to answer interviewers' questions, only respond to them. The following process approach can be helpful:

1. Choose a trait about your character or personality which is obviously true
2. Extend that trait until it becomes a fault
3. Put it back in the distant past
4. Show how you have overcome it
5. Confirm that it is no longer a problem
6. Stay silent

Here is an example:

- *'Well, Mr Jones, you have told us all about your strengths. Do you have any weaknesses?'*
- 'Well, I'm the sort of person who likes to get things done and I push myself quite hard. The trouble was, in my first management position, I would push all my subordinates in the same way. Fortunately, I learnt early on that not everyone gives of their best when kept under close supervision, and it was a good lesson to learn.'

Or

- 'I'm the sort of person for whom it is important to get things right, so I'm a great gatherer of information and details. However, I did learn early on in my management career that it is sometimes more important to make the decision than to go on collecting facts. It is a difficult balancing act but I manage my need for detail very well now.'

You can see that by leading with a strength it preconditions the interviewer. In the above example, it is important to get things done or get things right so your weakness will be accepted.

Notice too that the question always comes in the plural: have you any weaknesses? Only ever admit to one and let them specifically ask for another. In my experience, interviewers do not ask candidates for a litany of their sins and omissions. If you do get asked for another, confess to 'working too hard' or 'being over committed'.

CHAPTER 40

Multiple Questions

You will know if you have an inexperienced interviewer because he or she will fire at you several questions at once.

In such cases, remember that you have been given a choice and you can choose which of the questions you wish to answer. Usually, after your interviewer has asked two or three supplementary questions to your original answer it is likely that he or she will go back to one of the original two or three questions. So exercise your right of choice to your advantage.

However, if you have a professional interviewer, (you will recognize this by the constant flow of open questions interspersed with a sudden multiple question), then you use a different tack. There is a school of interviewing which suggests that an answer to a triple question gives an indication of the intelligence of the applicant:

- Answer one question = average ability
- Answer two questions = above average
- Answer three questions = very bright

An example would be:

'How has your job changed in the last three years, how have you managed the changes and what are the implications for the future?'

A good strategy here is to hold all the points in your mind by repeating the question.

CHAPTER 41

The Topical Question

Personnel interviewers are trained to discover what they can about you, not just as an employee but as a person. The two most popular ways of doing this are asking you either about what you do in your free time (see the section on interests on page 81) or what has taken your interest in the news lately.

The theory is that what takes your interest will in some way hint at your values, motivations and in some cases your belief systems. It is difficult to discuss Northern Ireland, world starvation or the greenhouse effect and not reveal something about yourself.

The 'topical' questions can also indicate how rounded a person you are, and whether you are able to see beyond the confines of the world of work.

Now that you know what lies behind the question, you can anticipate it and prepare topics and answers.

For obvious reasons, it is very important for you to give pros and cons on both sides of an argument and/or be able to speak to the issues, principles or viewpoints of the major protagonists. This will not only show that you are an informed person but also that you:

- See both sides of an argument
- Are fluent
- Are balanced
- Can make a judgement

Most employers would be very pleased to have employees who could display these talents in the performance of their jobs.

Some topics are almost predictable, for example:

- Oil companies – The Greenhouse effect
- Pharmaceuticals – Animal rights
- Local Government – Privatization
- Retailing – The inflation rate
- Customs & Excise – The Channel Tunnel

With a little thought you can probably predict three possible topic areas.

CHAPTER 42

Interests

Someone once said, 'Play is just as hard as work but we don't get paid for it'. The reason for this is obvious – we enjoy doing it. It is because we enjoy doing something that makes this such a fascinating question area for interviewers. What someone does with his or her disposable time can reveal to the interviewer so much about that person's individual talents, skills and natural motivations. For instance, take two people doing the same job. One in his spare time goes walking, collects stamps and breeds tropical fish. The other plays squash, belongs to a Rotary club and is interested in amateur dramatics. Their approach to the job and style of work is likely to be highly different and, depending on the organizations culture, one is more likely to be suitable than the other.

So whilst at one level what an individual does with spare time is no concern of the employer, at another level it is. The majority of us are not schizoid – we don't change our personalities once we leave work. Those who are high achievers at work are high achievers in their leisure. Those who are social at work will be social in their leisure time.

Thus the wise interviewee will anticipate and prepare

for questions about interests. This is particularly important for young candidates and recent graduates because there is not much on the experience side that the interviewer can use to make predictions about job performance.

It is also important not to give the impression, through having so many interests, that your main reason for working is to fund them.

Where possible it is appropriate to show you have interests that indicate you are social, intellectual and achievement-orientated.

Particularly impressive is where an individual has been elected or voted into an honorary position, for it shows peer group acceptance of the individual. It also shows that he or she must have organizational and persuasive skills which are immediately transferable to any management or executive position, and thus useful to a potential employer.

Questions to anticipate are:

- What do you do in your spare time?
- Why do you do that?
- What satisfaction does it give you?
- How long have you had that interest?
- What have you achieved through that interest?

There is a danger when you share a common interest with your interviewer that you may burn up valuable time talking about your interests and not the skills and experience which make you suitable for the position on offer. This means that you must become adept at constantly bringing back the conversation to work, or showing how your interests help you at work.

CHAPTER 43

Have You Any Questions For Us?

This is usually asked at the end of the interview and it is fraught with danger.

Danger 1: Is it a genuine invitation for a question or is the interviewer only being polite? If it is genuine, and only you will be able to tell, then go ahead, but if not just thank the interviewer for his or her time and confirm your continuing interest in the position.

Danger 2: Some research has suggested that applicants are more likely to be rejected if they break out of the role of interviewee and interview the interviewer by asking for information, opinions or suggestions.

The recommended strategy is as follows. Now that you have been interviewed, you should have a clearer idea of what the employers are looking for, so you can hone your 30-word statement to match their needs with your skills and experience (see page 18). You can also take advantage of a sales technique called the 'Assumptive Close'. This assumes that you have the sale – in your case that you have the job on offer. So on being asked 'Have you any questions for us?', your reply can be something along the following lines:

- Yes. But may I say how much I have enjoyed our

discussion (it costs nothing to be polite) and I would like to say now that I am definitely interested in joining you (shows you are motivated) because ....
....
(amended 30-word statement).

Now the question I would like to ask is 'What would be the key result areas of the job in the first six months?' or (being more aggressive):

- 'What would you expect me to achieve in the first six months after the appointment?' (Assumptive Close)

The advantage of this question is that it gets you off the job description which is usually prepared by personnel and into job targets which is why the job really exists.

An additional advantage is that you can then pull out anything from your experience that you have not had an opportunity to talk about but has a direct bearing on the specified key result areas. You can then say:

'Thank you. That has been very helpful, perhaps then it would be helpful for you to know that in 19xx I . . .' (tell the story of your experience)

What you have successfully done is:

- Not broken role as the interviewee
- Been able to extend the interview
- Got across evidence about yourself that is directly relevant to the real job
- Concluded the interview on a positive note

PART FOUR

THE 100 MOST POPULAR QUESTIONS ASKED BY INTERVIEWERS

CHAPTER 44

100 Popular QuestionS

These are the most popular questions asked by interviewers apart from the appropriate technical questions about your specific skills and experience.

As an exercise it is well worth writing out answers for each question rather than just thinking them through. There is a real difference between knowing what you want to say and being able to deliver a satisfactory answer despite the anxiety of the interview.

Obviously, it cannot be guaranteed that you will be asked any of these questions but if you practise (see page 16), you can go to the interview with the confidence that whatever you are asked you will be able to respond positively.

100 QUESTIONS

1. Why do you want this job?
2. Tell me about yourself?
3. Why should we hire you?
4. What is your major achievement?
5. What do you consider yourself good at doing?
6. What sort of person are you?

7. What are your strengths?
8. What are your weaknesses?
9. What do you know about our organization?
10. How would you approach this job?
11. How do you get things done?
12. How do you manage your staff?
13. What do you look for in a manager?
14. What do you look for in a subordinate?
15. How do you decide on your objectives?
16. How do you manage your day?
17. What interests you most in your work?
18. What have you read recently that has taken your interest?
19. What sort of things do you like to delegate?
20. What do you do in your spare time?
21. In what environment do you work best?
22. How did you change the job?
23. What motivates you?
24. If you could change your current job in any way how would you do it?
25. If you could change your organization in any way how would you do it?
26. How have you changed over the last five years?
27. Where do you see yourself going in the next five years?
28. Describe a time when you felt you were doing well.
29. Describe a time when you felt that things were not going too well.
30. How do you work in a team?
31. What contribution do you make to a team?
32. What would your colleagues say about you?
33. How would your boss describe your work?
34. Describe your ideal work environment.
35. Tell me about a time when you successfully managed a difficult situation at work.

36. When were you most happy at work?
37. Describe a difficult situation and what you did about it.
38. Who are you working best with just now? Why?
39. Who are you finding it difficult to work with right now? Why?
40. Describe how you typically approach a project.
41. Given a choice in your work what do you like to do first?
42. On holiday, what do you miss most about your work?
43. Given a choice, what would you leave till last in your work?
44. What do you think you can bring to this position?
45. What do you think you can bring to this company?
46. How do you see this job developing?
47. You seem not to have too much experience in xxxx?
48. We prefer older/younger candidates.
49. You seem over/under qualified for this job.
50. Why did you leave xyz?
51. Why are you dissatisfied with your present job?
52. Why are you considering leaving your present job?
53. Why have you stayed so long/for such a short while with your present company?
54. Why were you out of work so long?
55. Why were you made redundant/let go/fired?
56. If we asked for a reference what would it say about you?
57. What sort of salary are you expecting?
58. What do you think is your market value?
59. On a scale of 1 to 10, with 10 being the highest, how important is your work to you? Why not 10?
60. How did you get your last job?
61. Why were you transferred/promoted?
62. Do you like to work in a team or on your own?

63. What do you like best about your present job?
64. What do you like best about your present organization?
65. What did you learn in that job?
66. What did you learn from the xyz organization's approach?
67. How did that job influence your career?
68. If you did not have to work what would you do? Why?
69. Given the achievements in your CV why is your salary so low/high?
70. What will you do if you don't get this job?
71. What other job have you applied for recently?
72. How could your boss improve his/her management of you?
73. What decisions do you find easy to make?
74. What decisions do you find difficult to make?
75. How does this job fit into your career plan?
76. How long do you plan to stay with this company?
77. From your CV it would seem that you move every so many years. Why is this?
78. When do you plan to retire?
79. What will you do in your retirement?
80. What training courses have you been on?
81. What training have you had for this job?
82. On what do you spend your disposable income?
83. On taking this job, what would be your major contribution?
84. How do you get the best out of people?
85. Which of your jobs have given you the greatest satisfaction?
86. How do you respond under stress? Can you provide a recent example?
87. This job has a large component of travel/sales/negotiation/stress. How will you cope with that?

88. What support/training will you need to do this job?
89. What will you look forward to most in this job?
90. What sort of person are you socially?
91. In your view, what are the major problems/opportunities facing this company/industry/sector?
92. How did you get into this line of work?
93. What other irons do you have in the fire for your next job?
94. What will be your key target in this job if we appoint you?
95. What aspects of this job would you delegate?
96. What makes you think you can be successful with us?
97. What are the major influences that encourage you to take a job?
98. How does the job sound to you?
99. What questions have you for us?
100. Have you been coached in interviewing skills?

CHAPTER 45

50 Likely Interview Questions for Graduates

Milkround interviews are usually for screening purposes and consequently questions and the areas probed are general. The fact that you will have a degree in the discipline required by the recruiter usually means that the first question 'Can this person do the job?' (see page 56) has been answered. This being so, the thrust of the interview will be in the areas of motivation, personal style and interpersonal skills.

It is obviously not possible to guarantee questions in interviews, but the following pages carry examples from the four major topic areas together with suggestions as to the more popular questions. A good method of preparation would be to write out an answer for each question. If you do this you will discover that there is a significant difference between 'knowing the answer' and 'giving the answer' It is far better for you to discover this problem before the interview than during it! Writing out the answers will also encourage you to select the most powerful examples and words. It is surprising what nerves can do to one's fluency during the interview itself. Once you have written out your answers it is suggested that you practise them out loud (see page 16) so that your fluency at interview will be at its optimum.

The Question examples that follow have been grouped together into four major categories, but remember that interviewers will not always be as structured.

QUESTIONS ABOUT YOUR COURSE/DEGREE

1. How did you come to choose your degree/discipline?
2. Why did you come to this college/university?
3. What do you like most/least about your subject?
4. What class of degree do you anticipate gaining? Why?
5. How will your studies relate to your work?
6. How have your studies been funded?
7. Tell me about any project work you have undertaken?
8. What is your strongest/weakest subject? Why?
9. What have you contributed to the university?
10. What have you enjoyed most at university?
11. How does the approach to your subject at this college differ from that of other establishments?
12. What recent developments in your discipline have taken your interest recently?

CAREER QUESTIONS

13. Tell me about your career aspirations?
14. Where do you see yourself in 5/10 years time?
15. What attracted you to this industry/sector?
16. How will your studies support your career?
    (Note: This is a very likely question if, for example, you are a geographer who wants to be an accountant or a physicist who wants to go into personnel)
17. What are you looking for in a career?

18. Describe your ideal employer.
19. What are you looking for in a job?
20. What plans do you have to gain further qualifications?
21. Why are you interested in management?
22. Tell me something about your ambitions?

POTENTIAL EMPLOYER QUESTIONS

23. Why did you apply to us?
24. How much do you know about our organization?
25. Do you know anyone who works for us?
26. What aspect of your training are you looking forward to most?
27. Why should we select you?
28. What do you think you have to offer?
29. Where are you prepared to work?
30. What do you suppose are the main problems and opportunities facing our organization/industry/sector at this time?
31. Given your career plans how long will you stay with our organization?

QUESTIONS ABOUT YOUR PERSONALITY AND INTERESTS

32. How would you describe yourself? Can you give me some examples from your life to support your statements?
33. How would your friends describe you?
34. How would your tutor describe you?
35. What are your strengths?
36. What are your weaknesses?

37. What do you look for in a good manager? What sort of manager do you think you will make?
38. What are your interests outside your studies?
39. How do you spend your spare time?
40. How do you spend your vacations?
41. What newspaper do you read? Why?
42. What have you read recently that has taken your interest?
43. On what does most of your disposable income go?
44. How have your interests changed since coming up to university?
45. What motivates you?
46. Tell me about any of your sporting activities?
47. Besides your degree, what else do you feel you have gained from university?
48. In what societies are you active?
49. What positions of responsibility do you hold/have you held?
50. Apart from your studies, what will you remember most about your college days?

MISCELLANEOUS QUESTIONS

51. Tell me a little about your family.
52. What do your parents think about your chosen career?
53. What will you do if we do not take you?
54. What other firms/organizations have you applied to?

MANAGING THE INTERVIEW PROCESS

CHAPTER 46

Interview Start and Finish

Remember that the interview starts when you arrive at the car park or the reception area and finishes when you leave the premises.

So many people lose their interview by their behaviour before and after 'the interview' itself.

Secretaries and departmental staff are frequently asked their opinions of candidates, so your behaviour here is critical. Some older men have the unfortunate habit of going into 'flirt' mode which does them no favours. Relationships just need to be polite, friendly and formal.

Some interviewers make it a practice to escort candidates to and from reception. This is more than courtesy, for you can tell a lot about a person by what they show an interest in. One major national retailer has what it calls the 'staircase' test. Potential store managers are met in the store by the interviewer who then literally runs up the stairs to the office for the interview. If the candidate can keep up and not lose his breath he has passed the first part of the interview for a job where physical stamina is important!

It is the same at the end of 'the interview'. In my own experience I can remember saying to a particularly nervous candidate after the formal interview, as I was escorting him to reception, 'Well, that wasn't so bad, was it?' Only to get the reply 'No, and thank you for not asking me about . . .' The lesson here is that the interview is never over until you are out of sight and earshot of *all* company personnel.

CHAPTER 47

First & Last: Primacy & Recency

In 1979 three social scientists wrote a paper which suggested that final judgements can be unduly influenced by initial impressions. Since interviewers are human, they are not immune from the primacy effect. Once an interviewer has formed an impression of you it is often difficult to change that impression.

In popular language, you can only make a first impression once and consequently you must make the most of that very first encounter by

- The way you dress (see page 43)
- Your smile rate and eye contact (see page 52)
- Your body language (see page 48)
- Early use of your 30-word statement (see page 18)

You can draw a graph of what interviewers remember of an interview against times. You can see below it is shaped like a 'U' because the interviewer remembers the first impression you make and, of course, the last impression you make.

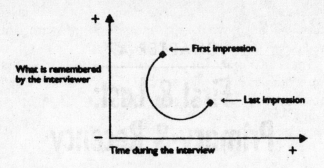

Figure 3 First and last impression

If you plot an interviewee's performance over time you get an inverted 'U' curve because it takes time for you to get into your stride and then you have difficulty maintaining your performance. Your graph during the interview looks like this:

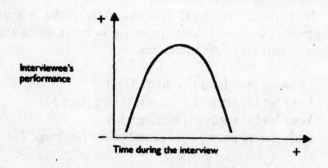

Figure 4 Interview performance

So you can see that when you are at your best, the interviewer is not at his or her most receptive.

In psychological terms what happens is this: once an impression is formed it acts like a filter in the mind of the interviewer. Only information which supports the first impression is allowed through. If information is given which is contrary to the first impression, it is either filtered out or diluted quite considerably.

Take advantage of the Primacy effect (i.e., first impression) and Recency effect (i.e., last or most recent impression) by starting and finishing your interview strongly. You can do this by the use of your 30-word statement (see page 18).

CHAPTER 48

The Interview: Arrive Early

How early is early? Well, about 30 minutes. There are a whole lot of reasons why you should do this, but here are just some of them:

1. If you plan to arrive early it will give you a time buffer against the unforeseen traffic jam; getting lost; not being able to park. If selectors have arranged to see six or seven candidates on one day and you are late, don't expect your interview to be extended. Your lateness will be interpreted as lack of motivation, planning or self-management.

2. Most people going for career interviews are anxious. It is not possible for the body to stay in high arousal for an extended period and you will find that the longer you stay in your prospective employer's organization, the more you will be able to relax.

3. Arriving early provides you with an opportunity to use the facilities, so at least you won't have that problem during the interview!

4. It will give you time to read additional information about the prospective employer. Large companies usually have copies of their house journal or product/service brochures on display.

5. Being early will give you time to take in the atmosphere of the place. On your way to the washroom watch and observe how people are working. Open-plan offices reveal a lot about the culture and ethos of an employer: look at notice boards, and read everything you can. You might even see the job you are going to be interviewed for under the internal vacancies section.

6. Finally, the previous candidate may not have shown up and you then have the advantage of an extended interview by being earlier.

CHAPTER 49

Divest

One of the reasons for arriving early is so that you can divest yourself of everything that is not essential for the interview.

It is only outsiders who walk into offices with their coats or bags. It is only salesmen who go into offices with bulging briefcases. Get rid of as much as you can. What you need in your briefcase for the interview should not be seen by the interviewer and it will include:

- Clothes brush
- Hair brush
- Shoe shine
- Peppermints

all of which should be used before the interview itself so that you can look your best and can create that all-important first impression.

What do you take in with you? All you need is a clear plastic folder with the following things in it:

- Company accounts
- Correspondence about the interview

- A list of dates when you are free to return for the next stage of the selection
- Copy of the CV that your interviewer has

On top of the plastic folder you should have a yellow sticker or note paper with the following written in very light pencil

- Your 30-word statement (page 18)
- Your USPs (page 31)
- Company information

Why a plastic file and not a briefcase? Employees walk round with files, outsiders bring briefcases. Why clear plastic? So that the Company Report will be visible and will let the interviewer know that you have done some research on the organization.

Why so little? Because there is less clutter and it is easy for you to sit with grace and leave in the same way.

Receptionists will look after your belongings.

CHAPTER 50

Watch the Layout

How you are expected to behave as an interviewee is not only suggested by the style of the interviewer but also by the way that the interview room is laid out.

There are three basic layouts used by interviewers.

- *Across the table:* the classic negotiation style, eyeball-to-eyeball
- *Across the corner of the table:* the classic colleague style with face-to-face discussions
- *Across open space:* the classic country club style, friend-to-friend

The range is from formal to informal and is usually a clue to how the interview will be: structured, semi-structured, unstructured.

It also gives an indication of the interviewer's confidence, experience and status. It takes confidence and experience to manage an 'informal' arrangement. The interviewer is relinquishing the trappings of status such as distance (provided by the desk), and comfort (interviewees have less comfortable chairs). It is an indication of status because it is only very senior people who have this type of furniture in their offices.

Since much of our contribution is communicated non-verbally (see page 48) the interviewee is most vulnerable in the informal setting. This is because the interviewee cannot hide behind the other side of the desk. It is well known that feet and leg movements are a far greater indication of confidence than what happens to arms and face. The interviewer has a distinct advantage when your whole body is on show rather than just the top half.

The main point of this section is to suggest that whatever office layout you encounter for the interview, let it affect only your style and not the content of what you say or your delivery.

Even in an informal interview, what you say should still be packed with your achievements (see page 37), and examples (see page 67). It is just that you present them in a more formal way.

CHAPTER 51

Do not Argue with the Interviewer

There is psychological jargon which is known as the second false assumption of Attribution Theory. Roughly translated it means, 'Interviewers believe that people behave in interviews the same way as they do at work.'

This is obviously not so because both you the candidate and the interviewer are on your best (or politest) behaviour. (The jargon for this phenomenon is Motivated Distortion.) This means that you would be unwise to take on the interviewer head to head, even if you felt it was warranted. Sometimes when you have a good CV which has got you through to the interview, although you do not quite fit the job specification, the interviewer may be quite challenging, and put questions such as: 'Most of your experience would appear mainly to be in . . .' or 'Your qualifications are in physics rather than engineering . . .'

You will do yourself no favours if you remind the interviewer that this information was on your CV anyway.

This is the process which you can employ to make yourself as attractive as possible without challenging the interviewer:

The Process:

1. Agree with the interviewer
2. Softening statement
3. State your position
4. Show how it relates to the specific need
5. Confirm that it is not a problem

The Example
Your main qualifications are in physics.

1. Yes, that is quite correct.
2. As an engineering manager I can appreciate your querying this particular point; however
3. my physics training has also assisted me in understanding the basic fundamentals of engineering
4. and my x years experience in engineering development have given me a very thorough practical understanding which I have always found more useful in the job of design engineer than the theory alone.
5. So I see a physics qualification as an added advantage to this type of position.

This section relates very closely to the hints on 'Reducing the Interviewer's Risk' (see page 62).

CHAPTER 52

What Happens Next?

No salesman would think of leaving a prospect unless he was quite clear about the next stage. You must be the same – do not leave the interview until you know what happens next and when it is likely to happen.

You need to know whether there will be a further interview, a medical or psychological tests. You need to know if this is the final stage or if you (and maybe your spouse) will be entertained to see how you get on in a social context.

Without this information you will be left in a sort of candidate limbo not knowing what to do or whether you should be doing anything.

Finding out what happens next will also show that you are not only highly motivated but also well organized, the sort of person who likes to know where he stands and can take the appropriate action.

It may also enable you to get that essential information for the next stage. Who will you be seeing, what is their name and job title, how do they fit into the selection process.

Remember too what was said about positioning yourself (page 35) and use this to get the pole question for the next stage or the offer of employment.

So do not leave the interview without knowing what happens next.

CHAPTER 53

Don't Eat, Drink, Smoke or Be Merry

You are going to be busy enough working out and answering questions not to mention sitting correctly (see page 49), so don't put yourself into overload by taking on even more tasks.

It would be unnatural if you were not somewhat anxious (high arousal) in an interview and this can sometimes interfere with simple eye-hand coordination (psycho-motor function). At best, you will cope, but when you are drinking coffee you are not able to talk about yourself – at worst, you shake and rattle the cup and saucer. In my experience, about one in 20 people at interview spill their drink in the saucer and about one in 150 actually knock the drink over because of their anxiety. Don't accept the coffee in the first place.

Don't eat either, for the same reason. Biscuits are fine but crumbs get everywhere and, in high anxiety situations, some people's digestive systems actually talk back to the interviewer!

Don't smoke. The interviewer might be a non-smoking convert, a health fanatic or have just given up. Even if you are offered a cigarette and none of the taboos apply, don't accept. High arousal does funny things to the respiratory function and coughing your way through your answers is not the best approach.

Don't be merry. Selecting a candidate is a serious business for the interviewer – remember what happens if he keeps getting it wrong. There is a time and place for humour but by and large the interview is not the place nor the time. Take your lead from your interviewer as far as humour is concerned but don't lead with the stories or punch lines. Remember interviewers, like lawyers and accountants, are in a risk-averse profession.

CHAPTER 54

Staying Silent

Interviewing must be quite a lonely job because many interviewers use the opportunity to talk at length to candidates. If you are fortunate enough to have this happen to you, do not worry; it will count in your favour.

Research has shown that the more the interviewer speaks during the interview, the more highly rated is the candidate! This is because if you are providing a sympathetic ear then you cannot be giving any negative information or contra-indications about yourself. So whilst the interviewer is talking, it can only be positive as far as you are concerned.

There is, however, a significant danger. Being an empathetic listener will only impress the interviewer as to how nice you are as a person, not how good you may be as a potential employee. If you are not careful, at the end of the interview you will be thought of as a nice person but there will not be much to commend you to the job. This is where the 30-word statement comes yet again to the rescue. You must not leave the interview without the delivery of the 30-word statement. For example:

Mr Jones, I have so much enjoyed meeting you and our

discussion. Thank you for telling me all about . . . May I, before I leave, confirm my interest in the position because (30-word statement).

As the interviewer has no negative information about you since you, because of being a listener, have not given any and because he approves of you because you listened, your chances are good. If the only information he has is your 30-word statement and he treats all the other candidates in the same way, then your rating in the selection stakes must be very high indeed.

CHAPTER 55

Avoid DTBs (Defensive Tactical Behaviours)

Remembering that interviewers eat what you feed them, so avoid mentioning negative information about yourself or your work. It is surprising how many candidates actually lead interviewers into this type of area hoping to be saved the Defensive Tactical Behaviours (DTBs) such as making excuses, offering prepared justifications and/or apologies.

Employ DTBs only when you have to, and that is only under direct questioning. Wherever possible, provide a justification and end it on the most positive note you can. There is a school of philosophy that suggests everything happens for a purpose and that good comes out of difficult situations.

Here is an example first of avoidance and then of 'coat-tailing' positive information on to the negative.

- *'How is your health?'*
  'It is fine just now. I enjoy good health.'
- *'Why did you qualify your answer with "just now"?'*
  'Well, last year I had an ulcer. I was off work for a little while but I soon recovered. It was during that time I decided to do my Open University degree and I started this January.'

In this example, the interviewer will hopefully follow up on the Open University rather than the possibility of a recurring health problem.

The use of DTBs is likely to maintain one's self-esteem because they justify personal inadequacy, but are not really to enhance one's employment opportunities.

CHAPTER 56

References

It is surprising how many people put references on their CV. with the assumption that one person can recommend you for any job for which you can apply.

Even worse is the referee who is chosen for his or her status rather than anything else. Commissioners of Police are useful if you apply to be a policeman or bishops if you wish to be ordained, but by and large the prospective employer is most interested in what you can do in the job. This means that the best reference comes from someone who holds an executive position in the industry or field you wish to join. A reference from a PR director for someone who wants to go into PR will cut far more ice than a local mayor or councillor.

You will not know which referee to give until you have been interviewed, because you will not know what they are looking for until you have been interviewed. The interview will tell you as much about the requirements of the job as it tells your prospective employer about you. Once you have been interviewed you will be in the best position to brief your referees as to what the prospective employer is looking for.

Here is the plan of action:

REFERENCES

1. By networking, identify good potential referees in the functional area you wish to join
2. Gain their agreement to act as referees.
3. Brief your referees as to your strong points and USPs
4. Give your referees a copy of the CV(s) that you are sending out
5. As late as possible in the selection process select and give the most appropriate referees.
6. Contact the referee by phone and tell him or her about
- The job, company and recruiter
- The major responsibilities
- The key targets for the first six months
- Your USPs for this particular position
- Ask for copies of references sent

IMPORTANT NOTE: Public sector firms usually require references before the interview; in which case it is best to advise your referees as much about the job as possible. Usually in the public sector full job description and person specifications are available beforehand, so copies of these can be sent as well.

PART SIX

GETTING THE BEST DEAL: NEGOTIATING PAY AND CONDITIONS

CHAPTER 57

Getting a better deal

The major reason why people move jobs is to ensure that they get a better deal for themselves. Once you have been offered the job all your preparation would be wasted if you were unable to secure an improvement in your financial position.

This section is dedicated to assisting you in getting the best deal you can for yourself.

There is an old adage that if you don't ask, you don't get. This section shows you how. Remember that employers expect you at the end of the selection process to negotiate for yourself. The iron rule of wages says that employers will pay you as little as they can to get, keep and motivate you. It is up to you to help your employer recognize your value and the contribution you can make to the organization.

CHAPTER 58

Pay and Conditions (The Basics)

The basic fundamentals of negotiation also apply to discussions on pay. The principles are:

- Negotiate only from power
- Negotiate only with decision makers
- Work to what they can afford, not what you need.

NEGOTIATE ONLY FROM POWER

When you are one of one hundred candidates you have no power, but it is surprising how many candidates at CV or covering letter stage state how much they are looking for. Often they are rejected for wanting too much, but the successful candidate may end up being offered more than he or she asked for in the first place.

Nor do you have the power at the first interview because being on the shortlist, you are still one of five or six. The golden rule is leave money matters as late as possible. When you are the final candidate, and it would cost the company a great deal to start up the process again, then you have real power. This is the time to ask for that extra ten per cent or that special fringe benefit.

NEGOTIATE ONLY WITH DECISION MAKERS

In selection terms this usually means the senior line manager and not the personnel recruiter. In most cases, the personnel recruiter can only say no; he cannot say yes without going back for approval so, whenever you can, delay discussions on conditions as late as possible.

WORK TO WHAT THEY CAN AFFORD

In large firms and for junior positions there are usually set bands for both pay and benefits but everywhere else they are negotiable, especially at executive level. Usually the 'c' circa that appears in adverts means ten per cent on either side of the salary quoted. These days it is so expensive to recruit staff that, at executive level, an extra few thousand is far cheaper than starting up the whole recruitment process again. However, to get the company to move you must not only delay discussions on pay as late as possible but also be prepared to negotiate.

CHAPTER 59

Pay Negotiation Strategies

Basically there are two main negotiation strategies to apply when negotiating your new contract – the Monkey and the Brooklyn Optician.

THE MONKEY

The monkey is the problem or the difficulty and, as the applicant, it is your job to ensure that the monkey is, as far as possible, with the interviewer. Here is a little demonstration of how a pay discussion might go:

- *Tell me, how much are you looking for?*
  (You have the monkey)
- Well, I know you are a progressive company with a reputation for looking after your people, so I'm sure you will be paying at the market rate.
  (He has the monkey)
- *Yes, but we have to start somewhere, so what are you expecting?*
  (You have the monkey)
- I might be tempted to overprice myself so perhaps you could tell me what the range is for this appointment.
  (He has the monkey)

- *Well, the range is between £x,000 and £y,000 for this position.*
  (You have the monkey)
- I see. Given that I have 'n' years experience and qualified in 'm' how high up the range would you be thinking of offering someone like myself?
  (He has the monkey)
- *We were thinking in the region of £x,000 + 2,000 to start.*
  (You have the monkey)
- [At this point you just stay quiet.]
  (He has the monkey)
- *But in your case we could offer £x,000 + 2,000 + N*
  (You have the monkey)
- Thank you. When is your first pay review?
  (He has the monkey)
- *It is in January.*
- Would it be possible to do something then subject, of course, to my satisfactory performance?
  (He has the monkey)
- *Well, we could let you have the full cost of living component.* [This has been budgeted anyway]
  (You have the monkey : You can either accept or go for more depending on how you judge the situation. If you decide on the latter, then say:)
- I really would like to join you because . . . However, I was expecting a larger salary.
  (He has the monkey. However, you are now sailing very close to the wind.)

The dance goes on until you agree a start rate.

THE BROOKLYN OPTICIAN

This optician sells glasses in the following way. In the right-hand column you can see how the price escalates.

The lenses in these glasses are very reasonable.

They cost only $40 (pause)	$40
each	$80
You can have the standard glasses but this particular frame costs $120	$200
If you want it in gold it costs $50 but real rolled gold is $150	$250
If you require the glasses within four weeks rather than the normal waiting period of six months this is a small service charge of $50 etc., etc.	$400

So what was quite cheap slowly becomes more expensive as the buyer is slowly taken up the price escalator.

The same can be done with fringe benefits. The lines show how the Brooklyn Optician method works:

- I presume you give medical insurance/at the London Teaching Hospital rate/for my family
- I understand it is an executive car/not less than three litres/fully expensed/renewable every year
- I understand there is a mortgage scheme at five per cent below base/You pick up the tax element/Can be used as a loan facility, etc.

Remember Rule Three – if you do not ask you will not get.

PART SEVEN

AFTER THE INTERVIEW

CHAPTER 60

Interview, Review and Learn

Every interview is a learning opportunity. However thoroughly you prepare, you can always improve. Treat each interview as a learning opportunity. Did you get the questions you expected? Did you answer the questions as well as you might? Did you help the interviewer as much as you could have done?

You should review your interview performance as soon as possible after the event so that you can learn from the opportunities it provided. Even if you get a PTD (Polite Turn Down), looking at the interview as a learning opportunity will help you get over the disappointment of not being offered the position.

If you do get a PTD it is always useful to call the interviewer and get feedback on where you were strong and where you did not match the specifications. Don't embarrass the interviewer by asking why you didn't get the job. Just ask for feedback on your interview. If you ask for feedback you must listen to it and not try to enter into a debate with your interviewer. Like all feedback, review it and where appropriate make the necessary changes.

Each interview that receives a PTD just brings you that much closer to being successful. You cannot fail at an interview because each interview provides an opportunity to improve and do better next time.

CHAPTER 61

It Helps to Stay in Touch

In spite of the title of this book, you can always improve on your interview performance. Immediately after the interview you should go through all the questions you were asked and review all your answer. There is always something that you could have/should have said about a skill or experience that you have. However, all is not lost, because you can stay in touch.

Three working days after the interview (usually too soon for you to have been turned down), write to the interviewer as follows:

- State how much you enjoyed the interview
- Confirm your continued interest
- Offer additional information about yourself which will help them in making their decision

This sort of letter works at various levels. First, it gives additional information about yourself directly related to the job requirements. This may be just enough additional information to tip the balance in your favour if you are in close contention with another.

Secondly, like advertising, it keeps your name in front of the buyer, namely the potential employer. You may have not been that memorable out of the six candidates who were seen on that day, but certainly you will be remembered from your letter. It will bring your correspondence and details to the top of the candidate file.

Thirdly, it shows motivation, commitment and loyalty to your prospective employer. If their first choice turns them down, who do you think their second choice would be? Obviously, the person who is keen to join the organization.

You can also use this mechanism for giving an additional referee (see page 120) who can speak directly of a relevant and specific aspect of your experience or skill which was emphasized during the interview.

This mechanism makes you appear keen and 'user friendly' and that in a job is sometimes more important than ability.

So keep in touch.

CHAPTER 62

Interview Yourself

The first hundred days in any new job are critical to your success in the organization. Most people in new jobs will repeat, in terms of style, approaches and behaviour, those aspects which were successful in their old organization. There is nothing wrong in this for it is sensible to repeat successful behaviour. However, success in one organization does not always transfer into another because of the possibility of differing styles, objectives or culture within each ambiance.

Thus the advice is for you to 'interview yourself' regularly in the new job, asking questions of yourself such as:

- I know what they said they wanted me to do, but what do they really want?
- How are people recongized in this organization and what do I have to do to get recognition?
- Who is thought to be the ideal 'corporate person' in this organization, what are they like, how am I different from them and do I want to do anything about it?
- What is my next career move in this organization and what should I be doing now to achieve it?

Postcript 1

Now you have got through the book you should be much better prepared for the interview. In the job search stakes you will, when you apply the techniques and strategies, find yourself with multiple job offers.

Your problem, now that employers want you, is to be very clear about what you want from the job and whether a particular offer will satisfy your specific needs. Here are some questions:

- Will the job meet my immediate and long-term financial needs?
- Can I or will I be able to do the job on offer satisfactorily?
- Will I be happy in this position?
- Will I get on with –
  My boss?
  My subordinates?
  My colleagues?
- Do I share the values and the mission of the organization?
- Will I be able to develop my career from this position?
- Will accepting this job help or hinder my long-term career ambitions?

- Is the organization part of a growing sector in the economy?

In making the decision about taking a job it is important to remember the formula: 7.5 x 232 x 42.

That is, the hours of work by the number of working days in a year by the number of years you spend at work. To put this into perspective, if you walked at four miles per hour for each hour of work in your lifetime you could cross the Atlantic 18 times. You spend a long time at work. Don't accept a job just because you got through the interview and someone offered it to you.

It is easy to pass the interview; the trick is to make a success of your career.

Postscript II

A question often asked both by individuals I work with and organization clients is about the morality of helping individuals through the interview. Is it right for the individual who is better groomed to get the job than the person who is best qualified?

The difficulty here is to define who is the best candidate. Capitalism in some ways is not unlike evolution: the better prepared the animal is for the environment it will encounter, the more chances it has of survival. The same with candidates in the job race.

My own view is that in a free society people can choose to do the best they can or just muddle along – it is up to them. If people choose to do the best they can at interview I would interpret this positively in terms of commitment, persistence and motivation. Most success at work is about perspiration rather than inspiration. Much of the information in this book is either common sense written large or publicly available in many books, and reading is not a prohibited activity. People can choose to take advantage of what is available to them, or bear the consequences of ignorance.

Postscript III

Another question I'm frequently asked is 'Won't the interviewer know that I have prepared and groomed myself for the interview? The answer to this is no. First, if you have read this book you will know more about interviewing than 90 per cent of managers, who will not have been trained in selection techniques.

Second, if you come up against a professional interviewer both you and he or she will enjoy the process. Try playing squash with someone who is unfit and does not know the rules. It is not much fun. Ask a buyer whom he prefers to work with – a trainee salesman or a professional. Ask a negotiator whom he prefers to negotiate with – a rookie or someone with scar tissue. Most professional people appreciate professionalism in another. Having read this book you will find yourself disappointed at the number of unprofessional interviews you will experience. You will enjoy meeting a professional.

Postscript IV

This is the most important of all the postscripts. The overriding cardinal rule is:

DO NOT LIE AT INTERVIEW

The whole basis of the interview is that both parties tell the truth. How would you feel if on joining a new organization you were not provided with the salary you were promised, the resources you were led to expect or the subordinates you thought were going to report to you?

You must tell the truth. But in interviewing you can be selective (please see John 19 verse 28). If you have suffered a recent mental illness and you are not asked about your health, there is no need to mention it. If you have been fired for incompetence and you are not asked why you left then there is no need to mention it. I don't know of any product, apart from cigarettes, that comes with a list of its drawbacks or inadequacies freely available at the point of sale. In my view lies of omission are permissible if they are no longer relevant to your likely job candidature or ability. There is an obligation on the part of the interviewer to be skilled enough to ask direct questions if he or she has any doubts about your ability or background.

PART EIGHT

CHECKLISTS

CHECKLIST A

Pre-Interview Planning

1. What do I know about the company?
   -
   -
   -
   -
   -

2. What do I know about the job?
   -
   -
   -
   -
   -

3. What do I know about the interviewer and the selection process?
   -
   -
   -
   -
   -

4. What is my 30-word response to 'Tell me about yourself?' (see page 18)
-

5. What points are unique about me and support my application? (see page 31)
-
-
-
-
-

6. What achievements will the interviewer(s) be most interested in?
-
-
-
-
-

7. What possible problem areas are there in my application and how can I put them positively?
-
-
-
-
-

8. What possible question areas will I have for my interviewer(s)?
-
-
-
-
-

9. Who would be my most appropriate referees for this position and what would I like them to say about my experience and achievements?

-
-
-

10. What lasting impression do I want to leave with my interviewer(s)?

-
-
-
-
-

The Interview Checklist

PAPERWORK NEEDED FOR THE INTERVIEW

- Advert
- CV
- Letter of Application
- Letter of Invitation
- Company Literature
- Plastic folder
- Pre-Interview Planning
- Examples of work
- Photograph

BRIEFCASE CONTENTS

- Hairbrush
- Clothes brush
- Toothbrush
- Nailbrush
- Shoe brush
- Peppermints/breath freshener
- Appropriate newspaper

Note: Remember to get rid of your briefcase with the receptionist (see page 106)

Feedback

Demands and styles of the job market place continually change. This book is based on real interviews rather than theory. Your experience in the job market as an interviewee (or interviewer) would be helpful.

Please write and tell us

- What you think
- Interview questions which you thought were good
- What worked for you and what did not
- Any points or tips you would like us to pass on
- What sections need improving

or anything you think that will contribute to making the book even more 'perfect'.

Send your feedback to:
Max A. Eggert
c/o Random House Business Books
Random House UK Ltd
20 Vauxhall Bridge Road
London SW1V 2SA